BATTLE ANGEL ALITA
ANGEL OF DEATH
Vol. 6
Action Edition

Story and Art by Yukito Kishiro

Translation/Fred Burke &
Toshifumi Yoshida
Translation Assistant/Lillian Olsen
Touch-up & Lettering/Mary Kelleher
Design/Mark Schumann
Editor 1st Edition/Annette Roman
Editor Action Edition/Megan Bates

Managing Editor/Annette Roman
Editorial Director/Alvin Lu
Director of Production/
Noboru Watanabe
Sr. Director Licensing & Acquisitions/
Rika Inouye
V.P. of Marketing/Liza Coppola
V.P. of Sales/Joe Morici
Executive Vice President/Hyoe Narita
Publisher/Seiji Horibuchi

Printed in Canada

Published by VIZ, LLC
P.O. Box 77010
San Francisco, CA 94107

Action Edition
10 9 8 7 6 5 4 3 2 1
First printing, October 2004
First English edition, 1996

www.viz.com   store.viz.com

CONTENTS

BEYOND THE YELLOW DOOR
Battle 30: Judgment Day

RMBMMMM
FACTORY 33
RMBMMMM
HUNTAH WARRIAH REGISTRATION NUMBAH F33-405, "ALITA."

RMBVMMM
RMBVMMM
IS IT TRUWAH YOU WERE THE WUN THAT USED THIS GUN?!
ANSUH NOW!

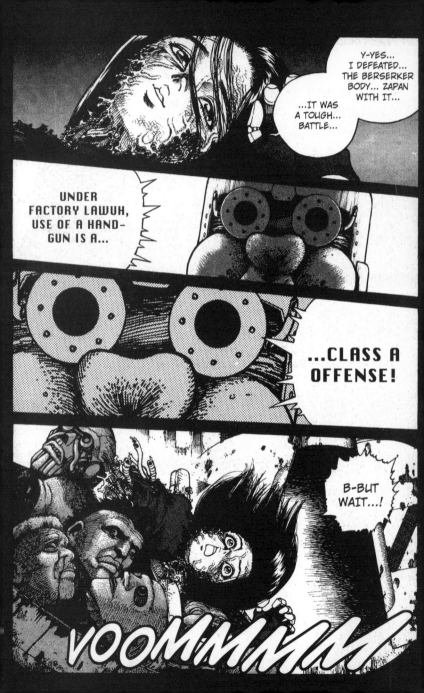

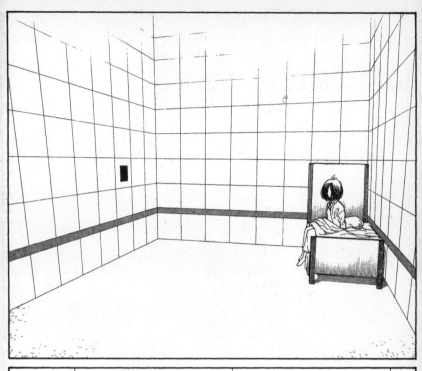

НИН...?

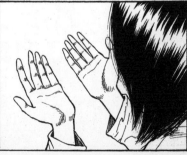

S-SO COLD...

WHAT'S GOING ON HERE...?

VOON

BEEP!

WHERE AM I...?

MUST BE JUST DREAMING...

HELLO.

...

WHO'RE YOU?

...CHATTING IN YOUR DREAM, AS IT WERE.

I'M SPEAKING TO YOU FROM TIPHARES...

THAT GREY ROOM YOU ARE IN-- MERELY AN ELECTRONICALLY CREATED DREAM VISTA.

TIPHARES...? DREAM?

IN *REALITY*, YOUR BODY IS IN THE FACTORY.

TAKE A LOOK!

VoON

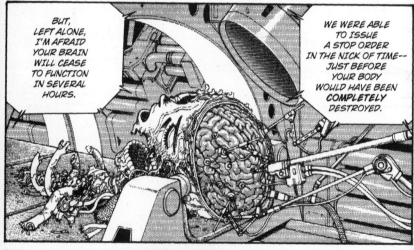

BUT, LEFT ALONE, I'M AFRAID YOUR BRAIN WILL CEASE TO FUNCTION IN SEVERAL HOURS.

WE WERE ABLE TO ISSUE A STOP ORDER IN THE NICK OF TIME-- JUST BEFORE YOUR BODY WOULD HAVE BEEN *COMPLETELY* DESTROYED.

W-WHY ARE YOU SHOWING ME THIS...?

JUST WHO *ARE* YOU?!

. . .

BASICALLY, YOU ARE *DYING*.

AND IN RETURN?

I CAN GIVE YOU A NEW BODY... A SECOND CHANCE.

I CAN CLEAR YOU OF THAT CLASS A CRIME.

I CAN SAVE YOUR LIFE.

HMPH!

WHY, YOU'LL WORK FOR THE GOOD OF TIPHARES, OF COURSE.

VMMMM

IT'S A SPECIAL DUTY A DECKMAN CANNOT PERFORM.

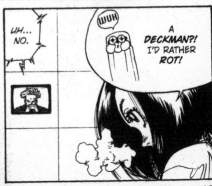

UH... NO.

WUH

A DECKMAN?! I'D RATHER ROT!

WE HAVE BEEN MONITORING YOUR ACTIONS OF THE LAST TWO YEARS THROUGH THE EYES OF THE TR-55.

K-KIMJI?!

IN ORDER TO FIND CANDIDATES FOR THIS PROJECT, WE SENT OUT A THOUSAND OF THE TR-55 ARTIFICIAL LIFE FORMS TO THE SURFACE.

WE'VE FOUND YOUR EXTRAORDINARY FIGHTING ABILITY TO BE MOST... PRAISE-WORTHY.

ALITA

I CAN'T BELIEVE IT! KIMJI? A RECONNAISSANCE LIFE FORM...?!

YOUR DREAM WON'T LAST FOR LONG.

...THEN OPEN THAT *YELLOW DOOR* AND STEP OUTSIDE!

IF YOU BELIEVE WHAT I SAY IS TRUE, AND HAVE THE COURAGE TO COME BACK TO REALITY AND *LIVE AGAIN*...

I-IF I WERE TO BECOME A "TOOL" FOR TIPHARES...

OF COURSE.

...WILL I BECOME... *STRONGER?*

YOU WILL RECEIVE THE FINEST BACK-UP-- IN TERMS OF INFORMATION, WEAPONRY, AND MAINTENANCE-- THAT TIPHARES HAS TO OFFER.

YOU WILL BECOME OUR MOST **POWERFUL** SURFACE AGENT-- THE **FIRST** OF THE **"TUNED."**

...A SCIENTIST WHO DEFECTED FROM TIPHARES... **DESTY NOVA.**

AS THE FIRST OF THE **"TUNED,"** YOUR PRIMARY MISSION IS TO LOCATE AND ARREST...

...DESTY NOVA... ?!

D-DES...

YES... THAT YELLOW DOOR...

HEH!

...BEYOND IT IS THE **ONLY** PLACE YOU HAVE A **FUTURE.**

I'VE DECIDED TO LEAVE THIS ROOM AFTER ALL.

IDO...

I DON'T KNOW WHERE THIS PATH WILL TAKE ME...

I -- I DON'T KNOW IF THIS CHOICE WILL BE THE END OF ME.

...OR WHAT AWAITS AT THE JOURNEY' END.

BUT...
I PLAN TO GO
AS FAR AS I CAN GO,
BELIEVING
IN MYSELF...

...WITH ALL
THE COURAGE
I CAN FIND
WITHIN....

FASHA

FASHA

THE HYDRO-WALL
A FOUNTAIN OF SUPER-VISCOUS LIQUID,
PROJECTED 20 METERS INTO THE AIR
BY A HIGH-PRESSURE PUMP, SURROUNDS
THE OUTER BOUNDARY OF THE SCRAPYARD.

ANGEL OF DEATH
Battle 31: Descent

FACTORY RAILROAD
THE "LIFELINE" OF TIPHARES, THIS RAILWAY CONNECTS THE FACTORY-CONTROLLED FARMS AND MINING FACILITIES TO THE SCRAPYARD. THE TRAINS ARE POWERED BY SMALL NUCLEAR POWER PLANTS.

AH, IN THE GOLDEN DAYS, ALL I HAD TO DO WAS PAY A "TOLL" AND THE BANDITS LEFT MY CARAVANS ALONE.

FIVE CARAVANS AND THEIR MERCENARY GUARDS WERE COMPLETELY WIPED OUT, WITH LOSSES EXCEEDING 40 MILLION CHIPS, MR. VECTOR.

THOSE GUYS ARE *CRAZY*... IN THE SOUTHERN TERRITORY, THEY EVEN ATTACKED THE FACTORY RAILROAD AND STOLE AN ENTIRE *TRAIN!*

BUT EVER SINCE THAT MOBILE BANDIT BRIGADE "BAR JACK" SHOWED UP FIVE YEARS AGO, THINGS HAVE BEEN A *REAL* MESS.

THE ONLY DATA WE HAVE ON "BAR JACK" IS THAT THEY ARE LED BY A MAN NAMED "DEN."

FOR THEM TO START ATTACKING FACTORY SHIPMENTS LIKE THAT... IT *THREATENS* MY POSITION AS A BROKER.

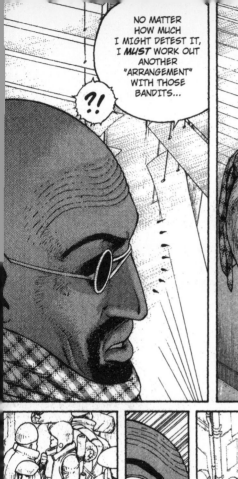

NO MATTER HOW MUCH I MIGHT DETEST IT, I *MUST* WORK OUT ANOTHER "ARRANGEMENT" WITH THOSE BANDITS...

?!

SEE WHAT YOU CAN FIND OUT ABOUT THIS *"DEN."*

THAT GIRL WAS TAKEN IN BY THE FACTORY AND DESTROYED MANY YEARS AGO.

A TRICK OF THE LIGHT?

UH... IT'S NOTHING.

IS SOMETHING THE MATTER?

YES, IT'S REGARDING THE SECURITY FOR THE NEXT TRAIN...

IS THERE ANYTHING ELSE?

SNAP

I'LL SEE WHAT I CAN DO ABOUT GETTING MORE WEAPONS OUT OF THE FACTORY. THIS IS THEIR BABY AS MUCH AS MINE...

DOUBLE THE PAY FOR SIGNING UP!

...RUMORS ABOUT "BARJACK" ARE SCARING AWAY MOST OF THE APPLICANTS. WE DON'T HAVE ENOUGH MERCENARIES TO GUARD THE TRAIN.

WE'RE TAKIN' ON THE FIRST FOURTEEN APPLICANTS!

BE ALL YA CAN BE-- JOIN THE RAIL MERCENARIES! HUNDRED THOUSAND CHIP EVER' WEEK-- MEALS INCLUDED!

THE LINE BEGINS HERE!

FOUR HUNDRED THOUSAND A MONTH... NOT BAD.

SOUNDS LIKE A GOOD OPPOR- TUNITY...

ALL YOU GOTTA DO IS SIT IN A TRAIN, AND YA MAKE LOADS OF MONEY! YA CAN'T FIND A BETTER JOB!

IDIOTS... THEY DON'T EVEN *KNOW* WHAT IT MEANS TO GO UP AGAINST THE BARJACK!

HEH... THOSE GUYS ARE HUNTER WARRIORS FROM THE *SCRAPYARD*--BET NONE OF 'EM'S EVER SHOT A *GUN*...

WELL THEN...

OH... IS THAT SO?

SORRY, WE GOT FOURTEEN ALREADY.

HEY!

KRESH

...NOW THERE'S ROOM FOR *ME*, RIGHT?

BWOOF

M-MY NAME'S *YOLG!*

J-JUST ASK ME *ANYTHING.* IT'S YOUR FIRST TOUR, RIGHT?

CHUM CHUM CHUM

I-I SAW THAT FIGHT YOU HAD... YOU WERE *GREAT.*

WANT *MY* RATIONS, TOO?

I-IF YOU MOVE YOUR GUN LIKE *THIS...* IT WON'T B-BUMP AGAINST THOSE SHOULDER BLADES OF YOURS.

YOLG, HUH...? THANKS.

HEHEH

T-TRY TO TAKE IT OFF--OR IF YOU STRAY TOO FAR FROM THE TRAIN-- AND THE EXPLOSIVES HERE'LL R-RIP YOUR HEAD OFF!

THAT'S ROUGH...

I-IT'S LIKE A NICE *DOG COLLAR...* RENT-A-GUNS *CAN'T* BE REMOVED, N-NOT WHILE YOU'RE UNDER CONTRACT.

THIS GUN'S GONNA GET IN THE WAY IN THE BATHROOM-- CAN YOU TAKE IT OFF?

H-HAVE YOU HEARD ABOUT THE **B-BARJACK?**

R-RUMORS SAY THEY FOUND A BIG CACHE OF OLD FIREARMS FROM THE RUINS OF THE LAST CENTURY... P-POWERFUL GOODS!

THAT GROUP WHO SUPPOSEDLY STOLE A WHOLE **TRAIN?**

M-MOST OF MY FRIENDS GOT SCARED AND DIDN'T SIGN ON AGAIN.

TH-THIS TRAIN IS HEADED TOWARD FARM 22. I'VE GOT A W-WIFE AND KID THERE.

S-SEE?

THEN WHY DID **YOU** STAY ON?

I PLAN TO GO HOME MYSELF-- *AFTER* I MAKE SOME CHIPS!

A *FAMILY*...

...HARD TO BELIEVE.

A LITTLE PLACE ALONG THE OCEAN-- OVER THE WESTERN MOUNTAINS.

O-OH? WH-WHERE DO YOU CALL HOME?

H-HA, HA, HA, HA! I-I'M NOT SURPRISED! THAT PLACE IS FOR *CYBERS*-- IT'S NO PLACE FOR HUMANS TO LIVE.

A YEAR AGO, WHEN I WANTED TO SEE TIPHARES, I CAME OUT TO THE SCRAPYARD... BUT THAT PLACE DIDN'T SUIT ME AT *ALL*...

KOMBINAT LIFE

VWOOO

SHOOOOOSH

GUESS THE
WIDE-OPEN
PLAINS
DO SUIT ME
BETTER THAN
THE CITY.

AHHH!
WHAT A
BEAUTIFUL
SUNSET.

E-EVEN THE MERCENARY CHIEF DOESN'T KNOW WHO *SHE* IS.

SHE ISN'T WEARING A RENT-A-GUN... AIN'T SHE A MERCENARY?

Y-YOU SHOULD STAY *AWAY* FROM THAT WOMAN...

H-HEY!

Y-YOU LOSE A YEAR OFF YOUR LIFE, EVERY WORD YOU *SPEAK* TO HER...

TH-THEY SAY SHE HAS SOME SORT OF LINK TO THE F-FACTORY... E-EVERYONE BELIEVES SHE'S THE "ANGEL OF DEATH"!

I PLAY THE HARMONICA PRETTY GOOD MYSELF...

HEH, HEH, HEH...

WANK

HA HA

SWONK

WELL, I USED TO BE GOOD-- AS A KID...

HA, HA, HA-- JUST WHO *ARE* YOU, ANYWAY...?

TUP

HEY, THIS IS SOME *RIFLE* YOU GOT HERE! WHAT'RE YOU GONNA DO, ALITA-- START A *WAR?*

SKUK

...ALITA.

THE NAME'S FIGURE FOUR... AND YOU?

...YOU'LL FIND YOURSELF IN AN EARLY GRAVE. HAPPENS TO *EVERYONE...*

YOU SHOULD BE CAREFUL, MISTER FOUR. IF YOU GET TOO INVOLVED WITH ME...

FEH... DON'T YOU TRY TO SCARE--

WHAT IS IT?!

--WHOA!

FSSSH

...

VUM

VUM

VUM

VUM

CHIEF, WE GOT COMPANY! *BATTLE STATIONS!*

WHAT'S GOTTEN INTO YOU GIRL?!

TOOMP

HUH? BUT I AIN'T GOT NOTHIN' ON THE MONITORS...

ALL MEAT Funk Flesh Girls BABES!

CLEAR AS CRYSTAL ON THE ANTI-INCOMING RADAR AND INFRARED SENSORS! HEY, HEY, HEY!

HOW 'BOUT YOU, NUMBER 5?

FOOP

HEAR THAT? NO WORRIES!

VROOOOM

OH, NO!
THEY REALLY *ARE*
ATTACKIN'!

UM UM UM

VOOOOOM

WHAT?! AT A TIME LIKE THIS? ARE YOU NUTS?!

CHIEF! STOP THE TRAIN!

!

WHAT?! NO! DON'T DO IT, YOU IDIOT!

A1 COMMAND TAKES PRIORITY! STOPPING THE TRAIN. WHEEE!

KREEEEEEE

SKEEEEEECH

?!

DAMN! WE WON'T STOP IN TIME!

NOOOO THE TRACK!

WARNING.... WARNING....

OUCH

ALARMS? OH, THAT'S *RIGHT*... I WAS THROWN CLEAR OF THE TRAIN WHEN IT CRASHED!

I WONDER WHERE THE OTHERS ...?

BRATTA

BRATTA BWAM

YOU HAVE STRAYED OVER 20 METERS FROM THE TRAIN! RETURN IMMEDIATELY!

BREEP BREEP

UUUNGH...

WE HAVEN'T GOT A CHANCE WITH THE TRAIN LIKE THIS!

YEEEE!

WAAAH! I'M OUTTA HERE!

WAAAH

IF YOU DO NOT COMPLY, YOUR ACTION WILL BE DEEMED AS DESERTION, AND THIS PACK WILL EXPLODE IN 25 SECONDS.

YOU'VE *GOTTA* BE KIDDING!

...

M-MY LEG'S BROKEN! I-IT HURTS! OOOOOOH...

HANG ON!

HEH!

YOLG!

W-WAIT... *PLEASE!*

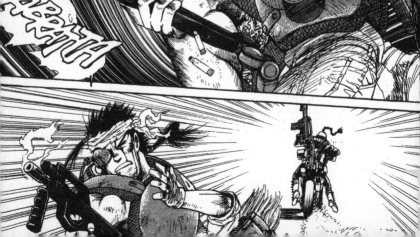

DAMN YOU! KILL ME! *KILLLL MEEE!*

TOOMP

TOOMP

...

I'M GONNA MAKE YOU *REGRET* LEAVING KNUCKLEHEAD *ALIVE!*

GOT THAT?! I'LL *KILLLL* YOU!

SHUT UP FOR A WHILE...

...

SNIK

WAAH!

?!

H-HEY!

THE NUCLEAR POWER PLANT-- IT'S GONNA *EXPLODE!*

LET'S GET OUTTA HERE!

BWOM

AAH!

WARNING... WARNING...

YOU TWO, HURRY UP! *RUN!*

AAAAAAH! I DON'T WANT TO *DIE!*

FWSSSH

SAAAA

SSSSs

RMBRMBRME

SHSSHH

PAP PAP

UFFF HFFF HFFF UFFF HFFF UFFF

IF MY OPPONENT'S A NUCLEAR *REACTOR*, THERE'S NOT MUCH I CAN DO ABOUT IT *NOW.*

FEH! TALK ABOUT *BAD LUCK...!*

VRKRRMSH!!

7αīん

VRMVRMVRMVRMVRM

THERE'S NO POINT GETTIN' CAUGHT IN THIS-- YOU'RE NO *MERCENARY.*

HURRY UP, ALITA! *YOU* CAN STILL GET AWAY!

I-IT'S OFF?!

!

KANGTANG

...IN THE WORLD **ARE** YOU?!

J-JUST WHO...

JUST SOMEONE WHO'S MADE A DEAL WITH MEPHISTOPHELES...

WHO AM I...?

82

BABOOM

HURRAH!

...

Y-YOU'RE OUR SAVIOR! H-HAHAHA! THANK YOU, THANK YOU, THANK YOU!

THE STARS-- THEY SEEM *EXTRA* BRIGHT TONIGHT.

HUH? THAT SHOOTIN' STAR LOOKS *FUNNY.*

H-HEH HEH-- DONTCHA *KNOW?* THAT'S A *UFO!*

...B-BUT I THINK YOU SHOULD STAY *AWAY* FROM HER! SHE'LL SHORTEN YOUR LIFE! R-REALLY!

Y-YOU GOT ME...

WONDER WHERE ALIT WENT...

B-BUT YOU KNOW...

TONK

SHE SAVES YOUR *SKIN,* AND YOU STILL *BELIEVE* THAT CRAP?!

THE GIRL WITH THE OCTOPUS LIPS...

GO...
AND *CAPTURE* HIM.

THE MOBILE BRIGAND FORCE "BARJACK" *MUST* BE BACKED BY NOVA.

G.I.B. CHIEF BIGOTT EIZENBURG

YO! WHY DONTCHA COME DOWN AND *EAT* WITH US?

ROGER...

YES.

WHAT?! YOU TELLING ME TO WALK THIS DESERT WITH AN INJURED MAN?!

TLONK

YERRGH...

YOU TWO WILL ONLY SLOW ME DOWN, SO I'M LEAVING YOU HERE.

I--I HAVE BE ON WAY

COME AND FIGHT ME LIKE A MAN!

I'VE HAD IT WITH YOU AND YOUR ATTITUDE, MISS "ANGEL OF DEATH"!

ALL RIGHT, THEN.

FSSH

FOR A "MAN" WHO BARELY ESCAPED WITH HIS HIDE INTACT, YOU'RE PRETTY LIVELY...!

THUMMP

KACHIK

HEH, HEH, HEH...

I'VE BEEN UP AGAINST THE **TOUGHEST** OF OPPONENTS, YA HEAR ME?! THE **ROUGHEST**...

DON'T YOU GO **UNDERESTIMATIN'** ME 'CAUSE I'M NOT A **'CYBER'** LIKE YOU, ALITA...!

KRUNK

FIRST, LEMME SHOW YA SOMETHIN'!

CANNED FOOD MISSILE!

HEH! THAT WAS ONE OF MY ANTI-CYBER MARTIAL ARTS* TECHNIQUES...

HE CAN USE THE *HERTA HAEON*-- WITH A *HUMAN BODY*?

TONK
TONK

I'VE DEFEATED THIRTY-FIVE CYBERS TO DATE! AND A *THOUSAND'S* MY *GOAL*!

YOU AND I KNOW THAT IT'S IMPOSSIBLE TO BREAK THROUGH A CYBER'S ARMOR! BUT *MY* BLOWS GO THROUGH THE ARMOR TO THE *INSIDES*-- CRUSHES YOUR *BRAINS*!

*ANTI-CYBER MARTIAL ARTS: ONE OF THE ASIAN ARTS SAID TO HAVE BEEN CREATED BY A GENERAL

!

WHAT ARE YOU DOING, AI?! LEAVE IMMEDIATELY!

HEH...

IF THAT MAN IS IN YOUR WAY, YOU HAVE PERMISSION TO SHOOT HIM!

I DON'T BLAME YOU FOR BEING A BIT SCARED...

DO YOU HAVE SOME KIND OF **BUILT-UP FRUSTRATION?***

CONTROL... LET ME HAVE SOME FUN OCCASIONALLY. GIVE ME A LITTLE TIME.

*ALITA AND CONTROL'S COMMUNICATIONS ARE INTERNAL AND CANNOT BE HEARD BY FIGURE.

THANKS, CHIEF BIGOTT.

ALL RIGHT, YOU HAVE THREE MINUTES.

...

I JUST CAN'T SEEM TO LET THESE TYPES PASS ME BY..

I GUESS IT'S TIME FOR ME TO GET SERIOUS.

I WAS A LITTLE CARELESS, THAT'S ALL.

HA, HA... WHAT'S WRONG?

ONCE I GET *THAT* CLOSE, MY TECHNIQUES ARE UNBEATABLE!

ONE STEP CLOSER AND I'LL BE IN EFFECTIVE RANGE FOR THE TEAI* ATTACKS!

SHOOO

PEEK-A-BOO!

TOOF TASHOOF

"TEAI"--IN FIGURE'S MARTIAL ARTS (KOPPO), MANY ATTACKS ARE BASED ON OPEN PALMED STRIKES (SHODA) WHICH

NOO

GRRR...

TUP

HEH.
NOW,
DO YOU
GIVE UP?

I WILL
NOT!

SKRAAA

FEH! I GUESS
I'LL JUST HAVE
TO SHOW YOU
THE *TRUE* EXTENT
OF MY POWER!

YOU
JUST
WON'T
QUIT,
WILL
YOU?

TMP

...ST-STORM'S COMING IN... OH, PLEASE, *DON'T* COME...

C-COLD... I DON'T LIKE THE WAY THOSE CL-CLOUDS ARE LOOKING...

SHAAAZAAAA

SHAAA

FSHT SPSHT

H-HE'D BETTER NOT BE H-HAVING FUN WITH THAT GIRL...

WH-WHAT'S TAKING FIGURE SO LONG...?

SPLORK

ZUHN

HEH, HEH, HEH. DON'T YOU SEE? YOU CAN'T DEFEAT *ME*...

WHY WON'T YO ACCEPT THE FA THAT YOU'VE LOST?

HEH, HEH, HEH. YOU'RE NOT SO TOUGH...

SPAK.

HEH! I WON'T LOSE.

FRAAAK

KRAK

DO I HAVE TO KILL YOU FOR YOU TO UNDER-STAND?!

HE'S UNBELIEVABLE.

TRP

SLRP

BOOM

WAAARGH! I'M NOT BEATEN YET!

SH-SHE'S LONG GONE!

SHOOP

HOW *DARE* YOU RUN OUT ON OUR FIGHT, ALITA?!

TH-THAT GIRL HAS NO BLOOD OR TEARS... SHE'S LEFT US OUT H-HERE IN THE MIDDLE OF *NOWHERE* WITH ONLY A *PITTANCE* OF FOOD AND W-WATER...

URWOOOOOO

FIGURE FOUR...

...WHAT A NUT...

PPLER RADAR AS PICKED UP DANGEROUS WEATHER FORMATIONS IN YOUR AREA.

NOW LEAVE THAT SECTOR IMMEDIATELY!

...

SEEMS LIKE YOU HAD FUN, AI.

THE HIGH PRESSURE AND THE RAINS HAVE COLLIDED--

REATING GIANT RNADO!

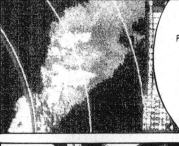

THE HEAT FROM THE NUCLEAR EXPLOSION AND THE COOL WESTERLY WINDS HAVE COLLIDED. YOU'RE IN FOR ONE HELL OF A STORM.

NO...

RADIOACTIVE THUNDERSHOWERS?

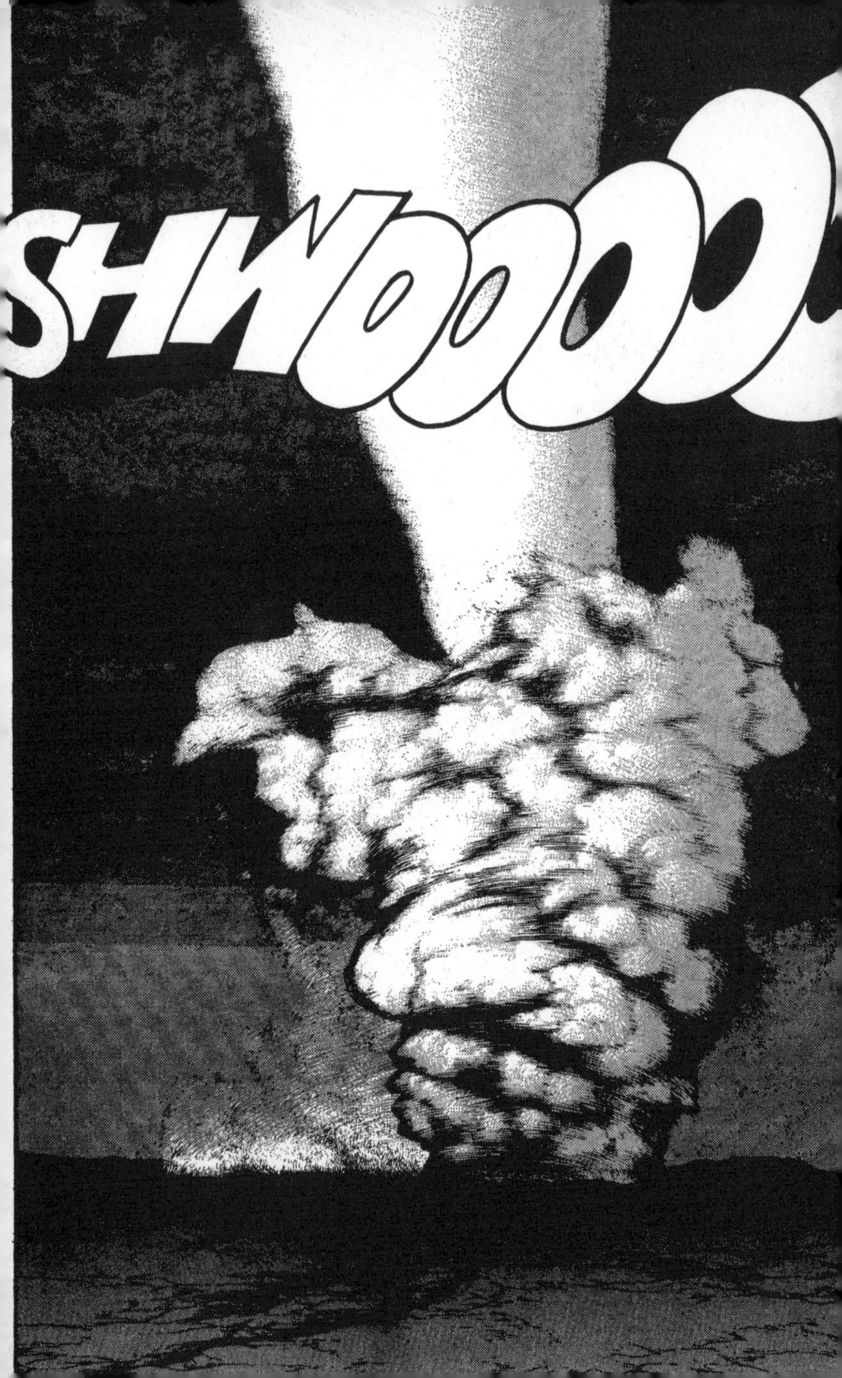
SHWOOOO

AH!

TOIK.

A-BWOOSH

AAAA

WHA...?
WHERE?

?!

BWEE

SHWAAAH

TALK ABOUT CLOSE CALLS! WHEN I CAME TO, THE JEEP WAS BARELY HANGIN' ONTO THE SIDE OF THIS BUILDING...

...IF *I* HADN'T GOTTEN EVERYONE OFF SO QUICKLY, WE'D ALL BE DEAD.

HEH, HEH, HEH. LOOKS LIKE YOU'RE AWAKE, ALITA.

MY HARMON- ICA!

STOP KIDDING AROUND AND PULL ME UP!

BUT SEE? WE'RE STILL ALIVE, AREN'T WE...?

...YOU'LL GO TO AN EARLY GRAVE."

"IF YOU GET INVOLVED WITH ME...

BUT I'VE *HAD* IT WITH BEING TREATED LIKE SOME *TOY!*

I DON'T KNOW *WHO* YOU THINK YOU *ARE,* MISS "MAYBE-I'LL-SAVE-YOU-NO-I-THINK-I'LL-LEAVE-YOU-BEHIND"!

WHAT'RE YOU SCARED OF?!

L-LET'S PULL HER UP, FIGURE...

...BUT EVEN WITH YOUR CYBER BODY, YOU CAN'T POSSIBLY SURVIVE A FALL FROM THIS HEIGHT. SO WHY DON'T YOU JUST CHILL OUT AWHILE?!

SURE, YOU CAN PROB'LY BREAK THOSE WIRES EASILY ENOUGH...

ERR...

CONTROL! DO YOU COPY, CONTROL?

DAMN, I CAN'T RE-ESTABLISH CONTACT...!

THAT UNGRATEFUL...! HE DOESN'T KNOW **WHAT** I PUT ON THE LINE TO RESCUE HIM.

LOOKS LIKE WE DROPPED THE BRAIN BUCKET SOMEPLACE! GIVE UP ON IT!

D-DIDN'T SEE IT IN THE J-JEEP.

COME T'THINK OF IT...

HEY! IS THE BANDIT LEADER KNUCKLEHEAD SAFE?!

AW, C'MON-- YA GOTTA HAVE A BETTER OUTLOOK ON LIFE!

THIS PLACE IS *HUGE!* WE MUST BE ABLE TO FIND FOOD *SOMEWHERE!*

O-OKAY...

F-FOSSIL-IZED CANS, MAYBE.

PLIP

PLORP

WELL, WELL! LEAVE IT TO A VET...

HEE, HEE! YOU CAN *ALWAYS* FIND WATER IN P-PLACES LIKE THIS.

S-SINCE IT'S A SPRING, WE SHOULDN'T HAVE TO WORRY ABOUT RADIATION.

POG

F-FIGURE!

WAH!

SQUEEK

SKWASH

HEY! THAT MIGHT BE TASTY!

I'M STARVIN'... THERE HASTA BE A RATTLE-SNAKE OR SOMETHING AROUND...

JUST DON'T LOOK AT ME!

TALK ABOUT ALL YOU CAN EAT!

--THESE CANS-- BRAND NEW...?

I G-GOT A BAD FEELING ABOUT THIS...

!

HEY! CHECK IT OUT, YOLG!

LIKE I SAID-- THERE'S A TON OF FOOD HERE!

SQUEEK

FWOOP

SHAAA

SO, HAVE YOU COOLED OFF A LITTLE?

TEEE

SHEE

I THOUGHT YOU MIGHT BE HUNGRY.

TASTY CORNED BEEF! MMM-MMM!

...I -- I'M SORRY.

FIGURE...

YOU HAVE EVERY RIGHT TO BE ANGRY.

LOOK, I'LL TELL YOU THE *TRUTH*.

RE *YOU* FROM ? THERE?

I'M AN AGENT OF TIPHARES-- THE FIRST OF THE "TUNED"-- ON A TOP-SECRET MISSION.

NO...

I *CAN'T* GO AGAINST THE ORDERS FROM TIPHARES...

AND TIPHARES SAVED MY LIFE.

IN A BOOK I READ A LONG TIME AG[O] IT SAID, "IN ORDER T[O] OBTAIN A SLAVE... YO[U] CAN EITHER BUY ONE OR SAVE THE LIFE OF ONE."

SOMETIMES I WONDER WHY I WAS EVEN BORN...

WHAT ABOUT YOU?

IT'S PROBABLY MARS... BUT I'M NOT SURE.

HMM...

...WELL...

WHERE WERE YOU BORN?

HEH, HEH, HEH... MY HOME IS A *REAL*[LY] NICE PLAC[E]

IT'S CALLED ALHAMBRA. IT'S A FISHING VILLAGE WHERE THE SEA HAS SWELLED UP, HALFWAY COVERING THE RUINS.

EVERY FEW YEARS, A 20-METER-LONG SEA SERPENT WANDERS INTO OUR BAY, COMING AFTER THE SEALS.

THE WHOLE VILLAGE WORKS TOGETHER WITH HARPOONS, AND THERE'S A CONTEST TO SEE WHO SPEARS IT FIRST. IT'S QUITE A SIGHT!

BEST YOU DIDN'T. YOU'D JUST RUST.

PFF.

I FEEL AS THOUGH I'VE WALKED THE DRY PLAINS ALL MY LIFE.

THE OCEAN... I'D LOVE TO SEE IT SOME TIME.

AAHH

HERE! SAY 'AAAH'!

...IN- SENSITIVE JERK...

IF YOU DON'T PULL ME UP, I'M GOING TO KILL IDIOT FIGURE HERE!

U-UH, YES?!

YOLG!

EVEN IF I *WANTED* TO...

...I'M NOT MUCH USE WITH MY *BROKEN LEG.*

B-BUT WHAT?

DO SOME-THING!

DAMN... I FORGOT...

HELL BEAST
Battle 33: Dog Eat Dog

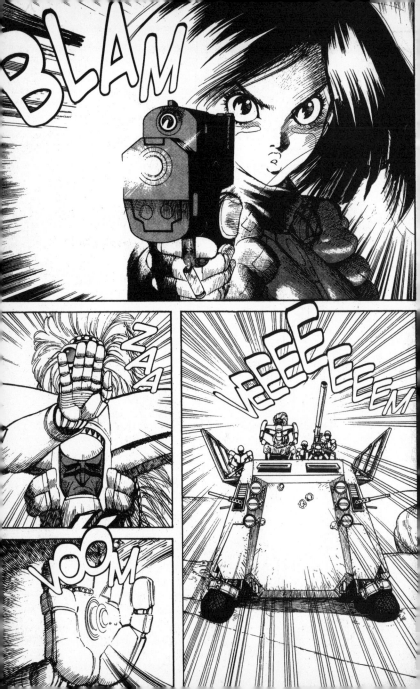

WHAT?!

HER BULLET WAS ABLE TO PIERCE MY TITANIUM-COATED HAND AT *THIS* RANGE...

...AND SHE LAUNCHED A COUNTER ATTACK *INSTANTLY!* SHE'S *NOT* A RAIL MERC!

?!

SPLA

BOOSH

BUDDABUDD

POOM

BOOSH

WAAAA!

AAH!

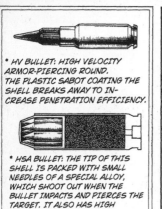

* HV BULLET: HIGH VELOCITY ARMOR-PIERCING ROUND. THE PLASTIC SABOT COATING THE SHELL BREAKS AWAY TO IN- CREASE PENETRATION EFFICIENCY.

* HSA BULLET: THE TIP OF THIS SHELL IS PACKED WITH SMALL NEEDLES OF A SPECIAL ALLOY, WHICH SHOOT OUT WHEN THE BULLET IMPACTS AND PIERCES THE TARGET. IT ALSO HAS HIGH STOPPING POWER.

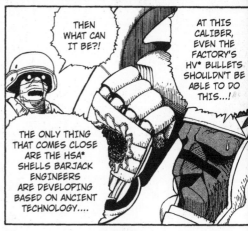

THEN WHAT CAN IT BE?!

AT THIS CALIBER, EVEN THE FACTORY'S HV* BULLETS SHOULDN'T BE ABLE TO DO THIS...!

THE ONLY THING THAT COMES CLOSE ARE THE HSA* SHELLS BARJACK ENGINEERS ARE DEVELOPING BASED ON ANCIENT TECHNOLOGY....

...IF ONE OF THEM IS THE AGENT, WE MUST STOP THEM *HERE!* UNDERSTOOD, SERGEANT?

WE MUST TAKE EVERY PRECAUTION... RUMOR SAYS AN AGENT OF TIPHARES NICKNAMED THE "ANGEL OF DEATH" HAS BEEN CHECKING AROUND AFTER US...

SSIR!

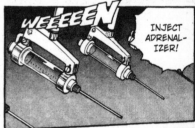

134

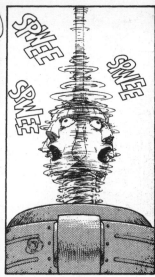

NOTHING CAN STOP YOU!

YOU ARE THE **ULTIMATE** SOLDIERS IN ALL OF SPACE!

SPWEE SPWEE SPWEE

NOW GO, MY **DOGS** OF WAR!

AAAAH! FEELS LIKE I'M ON **FIRE!**

MOVE OUT, MEN!

DEPLOY MORE TROOPS TO FLANK THE CITY...

SIR?

THE LESS THE WORTH OF A MAN, THE GREATER HIS PRIDE...

IF WE *ARE* UP AGAINST AN AGENT OF TIPHARES, HE'LL *NEVER* BE ABLE TO WIN.

HAH! KNUCKLE'S NOTHING BUT A DECOY!

DIDN'T YOU AGREE TO WAIT FOR HIS SIGNAL...?

UNLIKE YOU, HE'S GOT SOMETHIN' TO LOSE!

...YOLG'S GOT A WIFE AND KID WAITIN' FOR HIM, SO WHY DON'T YOU LAY OFF HIM!

UNH...

I WAS PROBABLY A *GUN* OR SOMETHING IN *MY* PREVIOUS LIFE...

H-HMPH! THAT'S NOT *MY* PROBLEM...

PIP

YOU'RE DEAD, GIRL!

CHIIIING

CHOOM

HEH...

SPWAM

VIIIPP

LOOKS LIKE YOU GOT LUCKY, KNUCKLE...

GYAHAHA

WOHOHO

WWAHAHA EEEHIH'H'!

BUT, COLONEL--*WHY...?!* I DIDN'T CALL FOR REINFORCEMENTS!

ERRGH! YOU USED ME-- AS *BAIT!*

PAT GYAHAHAHA!

AIN'T YOU *LUCKY,* KNUCKLE-HEAD!

HSSSSS

HSSSSS

HSSSSS

RELAX! HER BRAIN MIGHT HAVE INFORMATION THAT COULD PROVE USEFUL.

I-I CAN'T HOLD BACK...!

SLURP

I-I-I WANT TO SH-SHOOT, S-S-SIR!

WHEN DID THEY LAY DOWN BOOBY-TRAPS?!

BRATTA BRATTA

BLAM BLAM

MORE ENEMIES-- BEHIND US?!

BWOOSH

WAAH!

ARACHNO ※

ONE OF THE SPECIAL DEVICES USED BY THE "TUNED." A TIPHAREAN INSECTOID BOMB, THE ARACHNO CAN BE USED AS A BOOBY TRAP OR FOR OTHER TACTICAL USES, VIA INTERNAL PROGRAMMING OR REMOTE COMMANDS.

(AS STORED IN PACK)

BUZZZZ

THWIP

MISSIL BEES

BEEP

BLAM BLAM BLAM

BUZZZZ

MISSILE BEE ※

ANOTHER OF THE SPECIAL DEVICES ISSUED TO THE "TUNED." A BEE-SHAPED CYBORG MISSILE CAPABLE OF INDEPENDENT TARGET SELECTION AS WELL AS PRECISE TARGETING.

BWOOM

VEEN

VEEN

BOOM

..THE ANGEL OF DEATH" ?!

C-COULD THIS BE...

FFFFFS ST!

SKLUK

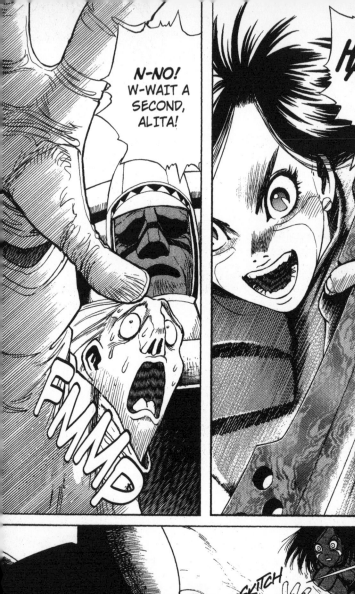

BRING THE **RESTRICTOR**!

FWUMP

KBANG

GAAA!

CALL UP THE REAR FORCES AND BEGIN THE RE-SUPPLY AS PLANNED!

REGROUP AND CHECK FOR SUR-VIVORS!

HFF

UFF

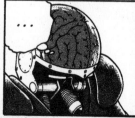

...

AAAHH...

GLUB

GLUB

" 'FREEDOM' IS TO TAKE CONTROL OF THE RUDDER OF YOUR LIFE..."

I-I'M SORRY, FIGURE...

FUP

"...YOLG'S GOT A WIFE AND KID WAITIN' FOR HIM, SO WHY DON'T YOU LAY OFF..."

C-COLONEL BOZZLE...!

WHAT ARE YOU DOING OUT HERE, YOLG...?

GLUB

TMP

177

HEH! THINKING THE HUNTER HAS BECOME THE HUNTED?

I-I NEVER THOUGHT TO SEE *YOU* HERE, OF ALL P-PEOPLE! YOU WERE SO PR-PROUD TO BELONG TO THE "GREEN BERET"* T-TRIBE...

I-I HEARD YOU WERE KILLED TWO YEARS AGO, FIGHTING THE B-BARJACK....

I SAW HIM-- THE GREAT LEADER, *DEN*-- AND I LEARNED OF HIS *AMBITION!*

UNTIL I WENT UP AGAINST THE BARJACK, I THOUGHT IT WAS JUST A NEW GROUP OF BRIGANDS... BUT AFTER MY DEFEAT, I REALIZED I WAS MISTAKEN!

TO BREAK FREE OF TIPHARES' CONTROL, AND MAKE OUR OWN COUNTRY, HERE ON THE SURFACE!

TO LAY WASTE TO THE *FACTORY!* TO DROP *TIPHARES!*

*GREEN BERET: ONCE THE U.S. ARMY'S SPECIAL FORCES, NOW A TRIBE OF HIGHLY

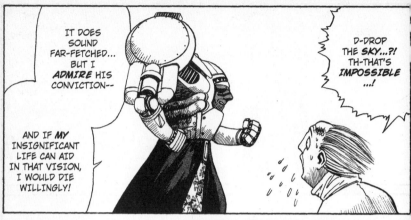

IT DOES SOUND FAR-FETCHED... BUT I *ADMIRE* HIS CONVICTION--

AND IF *MY* INSIGNIFICANT LIFE CAN AID IN THAT VISION, I WOULD DIE WILLINGLY!

D-DROP THE *SKY*...?! TH-THAT'S *IMPOSSIBLE* ...!

WE'RE ON OUR WAY TO ATTACK FACTORY *FARM 22!*

E-EH EHEH... I-I HAVE TO--

IT IS *DESTINY* THAT WE HAVE MET AGAIN, YOLG! LET'S FIGHT FOR FREEDOM, SIDE BY SIDE...

!!

P-PLEASE LISTEN...!

HMM... YOUR LEG IS INJURED? GO SEE THE MEDIC AND HAVE HIM REPAIR IT!

W-WAIT A MINUTE, BOZZLE!

F-FARM 22... TH-THAT'S WHERE M-MY WIFE AND KID ARE....

THEN GET THEM LOADED, DIMWIT! WE'RE MOVING OUT!

Y-YESSIR... I DID...

HEY, KNUCKLEHEAD! DID YOU OIL THOSE GUNS?!

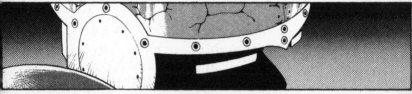

VROOM

VRRRMMMM

MMMMMMMMM

GLAAAA

GULP
GULP
GULP

ND EVEN
THEM
ULLETS
KEEP
VOIDIN'
ME!

AAAAH!
I FEEL
ALIVE
AGAIN--!

KACHAK

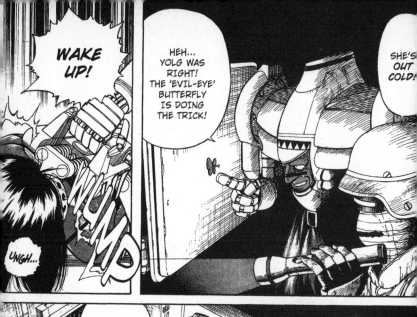

WAKE UP!

HEH... YOLG WAS RIGHT! THE 'EVIL-EYE' BUTTERFLY IS DOING THE TRICK!

SHE'S *OUT COLD!*

UNGH...

YOU'LL BE *THOROUGHLY* INTERROGATED ONCE WE JOIN THE MAIN FORCES...

...BUT THERE ARE A *FEW* QUESTIONS I WANT TO ASK YOU *RIGHT NOW.*

WAKE UP, "ANGEL OF DEATH"...

THAT MEANS... AS ONE OF THE *"TUNED"...* I'VE BEEN CAST AWAY BY TIPHARES...

IT'S BEEN *TWO DAYS* SINCE I LOST CONTACT WITH *TIPHARES...*

FORTY-EIGHT HOURS...

WHAT?

BUT... IF I'M BEING TAKEN TO BARJACK'S MAIN CAMP... THEN *THAT* COULD MEAN...

TH-THERE'S NO HOPE... FIGURE IS DEAD... AND MY MIND WILL PROBABLY BE *RAPED* OF ITS INFORMATION-- BEFORE I'M *KILLED!*

OH...?

heh.

PROFESSOR NOVA? *THAT* WEIRDO...?

MY PRIMARY MISSION AS A *"TUNED"...* WAS TO CAPTURE THE SCIENTIST, DESTY NOVA, WHO DEFECTED FROM TIPHARES...

HE IS OUR LEADER DEN'S GOOD FRIEND. I *SEE...*

IDO...?

THE TIPHAREAN DOCTOR-- PROFESSOR NOVA'S RIGHT -HAND

AND THE *ONLY* REASON I JOINED THE "TUNED" IS... IS TO FIND *DAISUKE IDO,* WHO NOVA TOOK AWAY...!

THE COLONEL'S BEEN SHOT!

READY THE SOCKET SOLDIERS!

WHAT IN HELL?!

TSSSH SSSH SKSSS

WHAT?

I TRADED YOUR ADRENALIZER FOR CLEANING DETERGENT!

PASHTTT

ADRENALIZER!

BNGG

SKLRP

GAH... GUUGH...

FSSSHU

FSSH

RABOOOM

BOOM

FSSSH!

BM BM BM BM

WAAHAHA!
BURN, BABY,
BURN!

BABWAP

UNGH!

YOU... YOU
SAVED ME,
KNUCKLE...?

DON'T GET ME *WRONG*-- I JUST DIDN'T WANT THE *OTHER* FOOLS TO KILL YOU!

KASLOOOOSH

HAAAAAAH! YOU'RE ALL MINE!

KLIK

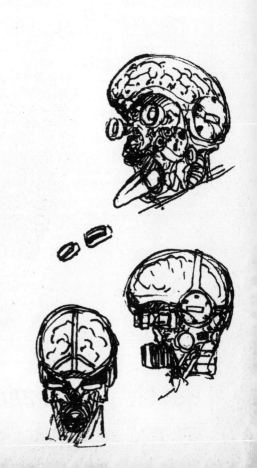

RAIN MAKER
Battle 35: Freedom Road

BARJACK MEANS NOTHING TO ME! JUST A *WORD*...

...*RIDING* MY MACHINE, *FIRING* MY GUN-- THAT'S ALL I'LL EVER NEED!

FOOSH

?!

SKI SHT

ONE ROUND--

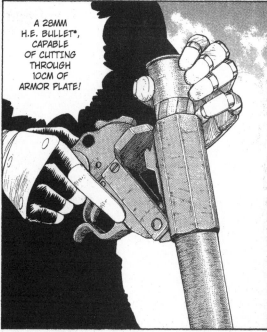

A 28MM H.E. BULLET*, CAPABLE OF CUTTING THROUGH 10CM OF ARMOR PLATE!

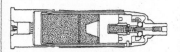

*H.E. (HIGH EXPLOSIVE) BULLET ※

(CUTAWAY VIEW)

THE FRONT SECTION OF THIS EXPLOSIVE SHELL IS A CONE SHAPE, TO ALLOW THE BLAST TO BE PROPELLED FORWARD UPON IMPACT WITH THE TARGET. USING THE PRINCIPLE KNOWN AS THE "MONROE EFFECT," THE BULLET CAN THEN PIERCE VIRTUALLY ANY ARMOR PLATING. THE PENETRATION POWER OF THE H.E. BULLET IS PROPORTIONAL TO THE CALIBER OF THE ROUND.

--BUT THAT'S *ENOUGH!*

C'MON, ALITA!

FEELS GOOD TO CUT LOOSE, DON'T IT?! TO BECOME A *WILD BEAST* AND *RUN* 'TIL YA CAN'T RUN NO MORE!

YOU AND I ARE *ALIKE*... I COULD *SENSE* IT FROM THE FIRST TIME WE MET! HAHAAA!

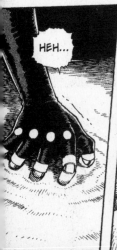

HEH...

LET'S GO, ALITA-- TO A WORLD WHERE IT'S *NOTHIN'* BUT *WHITE!*

THAT'S IT! C'MON!

STSSSH

HA, HA!

SKSH SKSH

HA, HA!

HA, HA, HA!

HA...?!

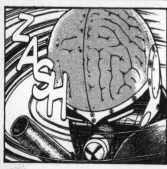

ZASH

WHA--?!

AHAHA!

HEH HEH...MY HARMONICA'S GOTTEN BETTER, HUH?

STS'HSH

BAD BAD

AHAHAHA! YOU JERK-- YOU'RE ALIVE!

OW! OW!

IT'S GOTTEN SORTA SCRATCHED UP, BUT HERE...

NO... YOU KEEP IT.

TITCH TITCH

F-FORGIVE ME... F-FIGURE... A-ALITA... FORGIVE ME...

I-I'M SUCH A F-FAILURE... A-AND NOW I C-CAN'T EVEN SEE MY W-WIFE ANYMORE... SO... PLEASE--

YOLG...!

UMPH

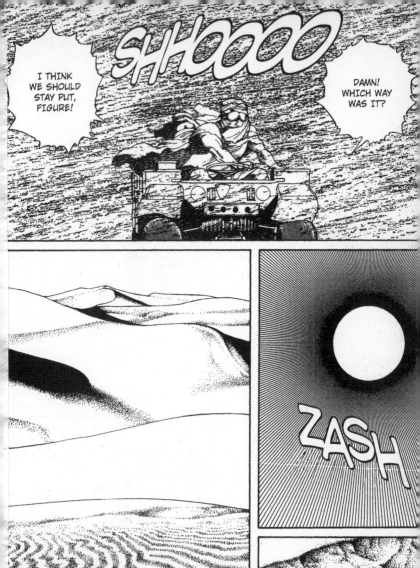

FIGURE...

HFF

UFF

UFF

YES, ALITA...?

FMP

US

* SOFT MACHINE: FLEXIBLE MACHINES UTILIZING NANO-TECHNOLOGY TO MAKE UP VITAL SYSTEMS.

NO, NOTHING...

DID *YOU* MANIPULATE THE WEATHER PATTERNS, DIRECTOR?

WHAT IS THIS...?!

THEN YOU *LOSE*, DIRECTOR.

I WAS MERELY GOING TO RECORD HOW THE REBELLIOUS ALITA WOULD MEET HER END.

...DO YOU BELIEVE IN MIRACLES?

DR. RUS- SELL...

...

YOU SHOULD RESCUE THEM.

216

FACTORY TRADE SYSTEM

EXPOSÉ!

Electricity to maintain Tiphares is supplied from space.

TIPHARES

THIS IS HOW TIPHARES MANAGES THE SUWFACE WORLD!

WASTE

Food, water, and industrial goods are sent to Tiphares via the Tubes. The Factories receive electricity from Tiphares.

Mt. Tiphares (1500-200m), a huge heap of refuse, collapses frequently.

INDUSTRIAL COMPLEXES

I MADE A FORTUNE ON THIS!

RECYCLING

Recycling the waste of Tiphares is the Scrap-yard's major industry.

FACTORY WAREHOUSES

SCRAPYARD

LABOR

FACTORIES

PRIVATE AVAN ROUTES

SURPLUS/ WASTE

ACTORY-ONLY UNDERGROUND TRANSPORT TUBES

Imported food and raw materials are processed and refined here. They are operated by the surface dwellers, under the absolute management of the Factories.

A TRUE STORY OF THE WALL

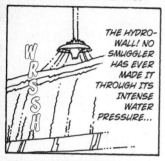

THE HYDRO-WALL! NO SMUGGLER HAS EVER MADE IT THROUGH ITS INTENSE WATER PRESSURE...

...STRONG ENOUGH TO CRUSH A TANK!

KREK

CRNK

PBTH!

NOW, GO!

NOT EVEN DYNAMITE...

BOOM

...WILL HOLD THE WALL OPEN LONG!

SPLOO

GYAH!

PLOO

GOT THWEE OF 'EM TODAY.

WRSSSH

THOSE WHO TRY BECOME PART OF THE FLOW...

THE END.

YUKITO.

Farms

The farmlands are under direct control of the Factories. Deckmen are assigned to the Stations, which the Factory Army and civilian mercenaries protect from attack.
Food is plentiful in the farming villages, but the scarcity of medical supplies, doctors, and cyborg parts is a serious problem.

Factory Railroad

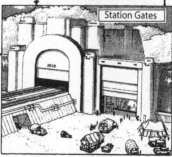

Station Gates

Eleven in all, they are under direct control of their respective Factories. Anti-terrorist measures necessitate rigorous immigration checks. This is the intermediate route Vector used to seduce Hugo.

Battle Angel Alita: Last Order

Creator Yukito Kishiro brings back cyborg Battle Angel Alita, along with some of her friends and foes, and introduces new bizarre, tormented characters. Desty Nova resurrects Alita in a biomechanical body, which makes her even more powerful. However, while she was "gone," Nova revealed the horrific secret of Tiphares. Killer robots are hunting down anyone who knows the truth about the floating city, including children. Will Alita be able to save them?

GUNM LAST ORDER © 2000 BY YUKITO KISHIRO/SHUEISHA, Inc.

Cinderalla

Junko Mizuno's delirious color illustrations incorporate elements of grotesquerie and politically sharp black humor. Her style has been described as "cute but deadly." Mizuno turns this classic story about class, labor, and the social role of women on its head with a distinctly post-pop consciousness.

© Mizuno Junko 2002

Neon Genesis Evangelion

Young Shinji harnesses immense robotic power when he enters the EVA; his mission is to save what remains of post-apocalyptic Tokyo. But the sensitive and complex teenager is more concerned with saving his friendships and figuring out the devastating enigma of his father, one of the world's top defensive scientists. This classic manga by Yoshiyuki Sadamoto and GAINAX explores nothing less than the nature of life, death, family, love and hate.

© GAINAX·Project-EVA·TV TOKYO·NAS 1995